Series Editor - Sylvia P. Webb

Sylvia Webb is a well known consultant, author and lecturer in the information management field. Her first book 'Creating an Information Service' was published by Aslib and has sold in over forty countries. She has experience of working in both the public and private sectors, ranging from public libraries to national and international organisations. She has also been a lecturer at Ashridge Management College, specialising in management and inter-personal skills, which led to her second book, 'Personal Development in Information Work', also published by Aslib. She has served on a number of government advisory bodies and is Chair of the Information and Library Services Lead Body which develops National Vocational Qualifications (NVQs) for the LIS profession. She is actively involved in professional education with Aslib and the Library Association and is also a former Vice-President of the Institute of Information Scientists. As well as being editor of this series, Sylvia Webb has also written two of the Know How Guides: '*Making a charge for library and information services*' and '*Preparing a guide to your library and information service*'.

A list of titles in the Aslib Know How Series
appears on the back cover of this volume.

Acknowledgments

I would like to thank: Birmingham Libraries for their permission to reproduce their publication, *Introducing Stock Selection*; Staffordshire University Library and Information Service for permission to reproduce a memo to academic staff; Joan Billingham and Marion Baxter of Sutton Coldfield Public Library for giving up their time to talk about selection techniques; and Liz Chapman, Librarian at the Institute of Economics and Statistics at Oxford University for drawing my attention to the quotation in chapter 7. Finally my thanks are also due to my family and my mother for their encouragement and support.

Contents

1. Introduction

One of the most fundamental responsibilities of any library and information service (LIS) is the selection of appropriate information. It could be argued that all other activities, from the enquiry service to the photocopying facilities, are either directly or indirectly dependent on the choices made. However the selection of resources has never been the simple task it might appear to outsiders; whatever the type of service – public, academic or commercial – weighing the needs of the users against the funds available has always been a major preoccupation of the information profession. During the 1990s however this balancing act has become much harder, as the selection process has become more involved. This complexity can be ascribed to a number of factors, partly technological and partly economic.

Quantity of information

One of the indirect results of the information technology revolution has been a large increase in the number of resources available. Part of this change can be attributed to the advent of desk top publishing, with its low costs and high quality output, but the main reason is the growth in electronic information – there is now an increasing body of knowledge only available in machine readable format. In addition a far wider range of information is now available. A few years ago electronic full-text sources were limited in scope to text and the occasional diagram – now with multimedia technology, sound, video, animation and interactivity are commonplace components of many sources. Whereas once numeric databases contained only raw data, many now routinely include software which will analyse the information and display it as graphs and charts. The statistics are impressive – figures compiled for the British Library Research and Development Department for example show a 400% increase in the number of CD-ROM titles published between 1992 and 1995.[1]

Internet

With its vast, diverse collection of information on virtually every subject imaginable, the Internet too can no longer be ignored as a potential source of information. If the figures for CD-ROM are impressive, those for the Internet are overwhelming – more than 5 million host computers connecting together 30 million people in more than 150 countries.[2] Much of the recent phenomenal growth can be accounted for by the advent of the World Wide Web (WWW), the hypertext interface developed to provide easy access to resources available on the Internet. However this growth has brought problems in its wake, not least the lack of an organisational structure for locating relevant resources. In addition many of these resources are not subject to any kind of outside control, raising issues about the quality of the information retrieved.

Delivery mechanisms

Another complex factor with which selectors have to grapple is the ever widening range of delivery mechanisms. From a time, in the not so distant past, when print was the main medium of information transfer, we now have a range of electronic options. At one level this may involve the choice between the printed and CD-ROM version of a standard reference tool, a decision which raises questions about the convenience of hard copy versus the enhanced searching facilities available with its computerised counterpart. At another level this may require a difficult decision on the most appropriate electronic source of supply. A few years ago networked access to on-line services simply meant the use of a commercial host such as DIALOG, with the searching conducted by an intermediary. Now a bewildering array of delivery mechanisms is on offer. The same information may be available via commercial on-line hosts, or – for British universities at least – through collaborative academic sharing schemes such as BIDS (Bath Information and Data Services), directly from the publisher over the Internet, or on CD-ROM. Nor is the latter option as straightforward as it may appear – in addition to the option of networking the CD-ROM it is now also feasible with a sufficiently powerful computer to download the information on to the hard disc, thus speeding up the searching process considerably.

Technological change

The planning and budgeting of resources is becoming much more uncertain because of the speed of technological change. While the CD-ROM market is booming at present, its long term future is more uncertain. Much controversy has centred around the technical limitations of CD-ROM, and the possibility that it is only an interim technology, likely to become obsolete as network access improves and the 'information superhighway' becomes a reality. If this should prove to be the case, how wise is it to invest large sums of money in installing or improving CD-ROM equipment and networks?

Access versus holdings

As advances in networking make it feasible to transmit much larger quantities of information to a user's own workstation, direct access will no longer mean simply the physical retrieval of items from a library's shelves. The development of electronic document delivery is beginning to offer freedom from an old professional dilemma – whether to buy material in advance in the expectation (or hope) that it will be useful, or to wait until a clear need is expressed and face the consequent delays involved in purchasing or borrowing the item required. Serials collections in particular are likely to be the subject of much reassessment in the future, with the growth of services such as Knight Ridder's *UnCover* and the British Library's *Inside Information*. These CAS-IAS (Current Alerting Services combined with Individual Article Supply) databases offer electronic, readily searchable access to the contents pages of a huge range of journals, with the facility to obtain copies of specific articles by fax, and in the future directly via a network. However this shift from 'just-in-case' to 'just-in-time' acquisition, is likely to bring its own difficulties in its wake, not least problems of user resistance and the open-ended nature of the funding requirements.

Electronic publishing

Though still partly at the experimental stage, two further developments which may impact on holdings are on demand and electronic custom publishing. The differences between these two developments are not very clear cut, but generally electronic custom publishing is seen as the selection of material from a range of sources, brought together and printed off with the payment of royalties to the publishers concerned – a development which is generating much interest in the academic sphere. On demand publishing tends to refer to services such as ADONIS, in which a very large collection of articles from a wide range of biomedical journals is stored on CD-ROM, with each paper being printed off and charged for at a rate which includes royalties to the appropriate publisher. While such methods of supply have clear attractions to librarians, the relief should probably not be too premature, as there are the inevitable copyright problems which must be surmounted before the techniques can come into widespread use.

User expectations

As with other public facilities such as education and health, many users now have far higher expectations of what libraries and information services can provide. A host of reasons could be put forward to explain why this might be so – the expectations raised by consumer charters, the pressures of employment, the need to acquire qualifications, plus a generally perceived belief that computerisation should be improving, not inhibiting, the access to information. Whatever the causes it is clear that needs of users are becoming increasingly sophisticated, while at the same time users are less able or willing to wait for the information required.

Funding constraints

Ironically these higher expectations are arising at the same time as many library and information services are experiencing much tighter constraints on funding – funding not only for the supply of resources but also for the provision of staff to utilise these. In addition in some subject fields prices have risen far beyond the level of inflation – for example the average cost of medical, scientific and technical journals increased by nearly 100% between 1989 and 1994.[1] This situation, plus the general move in all professions towards greater accountability, makes it even more important that selection decisions are based on sound principles which can be explained and justified if necessary.

Of course the underlying principles of resource selection are not different from the old-established criteria used for book evaluation, familiar to generations of library school students. However the criteria are becoming wider and more complex, as the unique characteristics of electronic information are taken into account. Choosing resources in electronic format involves not only decisions on the value and utility of the subject matter but also the selection of the most appropriate delivery mechanism and user interface. We are gradually moving from a position in which material was bought and kept within the library's walls, towards a hybrid state, where much information is not owned but simply made available via the service. This change inevitably raises difficult issues about how electronic information should be selected, controlled and integrated into the existing stock, since it is clear that in the medium term at least, printed sources will still form a major part of many collections.

The aim of this guide is to try to clarify the issues involved in the selection of information resources in both print and electronic format, and to suggest practical criteria which can be applied in the evaluation of material. It should be made clear at this point however that there are no 'good buys' – the number of resources which are an absolute must for every service can probably be counted on two hands. The remainder fall into the category of 'possibles' – worth selecting if the scope is right, if the information is sufficiently relevant to the users, and if the price is affordable. The questions may be similar, but the answers will inevitably be different for each service.

References

1. *Library & Information Statistics Tables for the United Kingdom*; compiled and published for the British Library Research & Development Department by the Library & Information Statistics Unit (LISU). Loughborough University, LISU, 1995.
2. *The Gale Guide to Internet Databases.* Detroit, Gale Research, 1995.

2. Consultation and fact finding

The starting point for any guide on the selection of information resources must be the users. It is crucially important to determine what their information needs are – the more that is known of these requirements, the better the selection will be. Users depend to a large extent – probably far more than they realise – on the ability of library and information staff to spot potentially valuable sources of information. An awareness of people's interests is essential when finding out what is available, and in filtering out irrelevant material. The same knowledge is equally important in estimating the likely level of demand for a resource and whether this would be sufficient to warrant purchase.

However finding out what the users of an individual service need can seem a daunting task to a newcomer, especially if the subject field or discipline is unfamiliar. While there is much literature about user needs, far less deals with the practicalities of how to make an assessment. Acquiring a detailed knowledge does take effort – although the most vocal users will always ask for what they want, finding out the needs of the silent majority requires a more active approach. Making this assessment involves a combination of approaches – some of which are limited in scope to specific types of service, while others are applicable across the board.

Users' requests

In any service one of the main methods is through the users' requests. Their enquiries – especially those for which it is hard to find answers – are often very good indicators of areas in which more resources are needed. One enquiry on a topic may not warrant a purchase, but when several users start asking for similar information, it is time to begin looking at what is available. A good memory jogger – especially in a service point staffed by several people – is to keep a record of the subject fields of the enquiries, or at least those which have proved difficult to answer.

Particularly in public and academic libraries another obvious source of information is the material requested by the users themselves, either in person or via the reservation and inter-library loan system. Essentially such requests fall in two categories – those to be bought and those which cannot be satisfied, either on the grounds of expense or because the information is of too limited interest to make its purchase viable. It may be possible to borrow those in the latter category, via Inter-Library Loan (ILL). Whatever the criteria used to make selection decisions, it is important not to deal with these requests in too mechanistic a fashion, or the opportunity to gain an overview of the type of material in demand will be missed. All requests are significant to the users concerned – whether or not these result in a purchase, they all help in building up a profile of the service's clientele.

In more specialised library and information units, the scale of the enquiries may differ but the same principle of monitoring applies. Requests for on-line searches for example can give a useful lead on the direction in which the activities of the organisation are heading. Carrying out a search at the beginning of a project can provide a good opportunity to discover how transient or permanent the interest is likely to be.

User liaison

It is equally important to establish and maintain good liaison with the users, via both informal and formal channels of communication. One of the simplest but most effective means of achieving this is to talk directly to the users themselves, whenever an opportunity presents itself. For example it can be a good idea to deliver information such as the results of an on-line search in person rather than using electronic mail or the internal post – frequently someone you meet on the way will also need information and the more contacts that can be made the better the service will become. Of course in a busy environment it can be hard to make the time to find out users' interests and ask their views, and painful to discover for example that they consider that most of the books on computing are out-of-date. However as an eye-opener to the needs and perceptions of the clientele it is excellent – the advice of informed users is invaluable.

In a commercial or academic organisation, establishing contact with the heads of sections or departments can be a very effective way of finding out the longer term direction of interests – making an appointment to visit these key personnel is a good means of introduction as well as effective public relations for the service. Giving a short presentation about the service – or a specific aspect of it – can also provide a good chance to gain feedback from users on their interests. In an industrial setting for instance it may be feasible to arrange an annual seminar with each research group, at which details of new projects are likely to emerge.

More formally, the committee structure in an organisation should give the opportunity to keep up to date with the long-term direction in which the institution is heading. In universities and colleges the agenda of committees of Faculty, School and other Boards of Studies will include plans for new courses and changes in the direction of research interests – of vital importance in the identification of future resources and a major reason for ensuring that the library and information service (LIS) is represented at such meetings.

Other sources

Although initially it may not look a very promising lead, careful scrutiny of an organisation's internal documentation – annual reviews, reports, house journals and such like – can also pay dividends. The progress of a research project will normally be written up in the form of interim and final reports, often the responsibility of the information unit to index and store. Browsing through the first couple of pages of these will help to give some idea of the scope and scale of the work. Internal newsletters usually carry features about new staff and their fields of interest – useful information which might otherwise take months to filter through to the LIS.

In academic services, reading lists are an essential element in determining what resources are needed. The problem, as anyone who has worked in this type of library will be aware, lies in extracting these lists from the teachers and lecturers concerned. Here an active – or 'chivvying' – approach will almost certainly be necessary to get results. When requesting lists, it is worth asking staff if they would categorise the items into the following groups – those that are essential reading, those for background information, and those which students are expected to buy themselves – to give some idea of the likely demand for each title.

Although time-consuming, carrying out a small-scale survey also offers a systematic way of finding out what users want. Obviously the normal caveats apply: the sample chosen should be as representative as possible, there should be no leading questions, and allowances should be made for the fact that users are not always able to explain what they need, or that their actions may differ from their words. Despite these limitations a survey can be a help in highlighting areas of need – users will not be slow to point out where the major deficiencies lie or what information is out of date or hard to obtain. Factual evidence from the users themselves is also likely to prove a good asset in any bids for extra funding for new resources.

Where there is a sizeable amount of stock another technique is to look at the usage statistics, such as issue figures and reservation requests. While providing an indication of trends and interests though, it should be borne in mind that it is *only* the use of existing stock which is being assessed. Analysing ILL requests can give some clues as to the material needed which is not available on site. In theory analyses of such statistics should be relatively easy to carry out if an automated housekeeping system is in use. In practice it is not always simple to extract meaningful information, without either being swamped by extraneous detail or spending an inordinate amount of time on the task. A less systematic but useful technique is regularly check the reservation shelves, the books awaiting re-shelving and ILL requests since these are items which are in current demand.

The option is also open to any library or information unit to solicit comments directly from users, via a suggestions box or by means of a pre-printed form. Inevitably some will be brickbats, along the lines of 'I have been waiting... ' – but hopefully there will also be some compliments such as 'Your staff have been very helpful...'. In terms of resource selection there will be positive outcomes, such as comments highlighting subjects where more information is needed or where extra copies of source material should be bought.

Summing-up

As an overview of the users' needs and interests is established, important points – about their background, work patterns, the way they look for information, the level of their computing skills – should emerge. It is vital that these points are considered when information resources are being selected – knowing for example that most staff in a university have their own workstation connected to the campus network makes it feasible to take out a blanket subscription to BIDS, the academic on-line service aimed at end-users. Equally in a commercial environment the fact that many users require only current information would be likely to preclude buying a CD-ROM which is updated only twice a year. The aim is to chose those resources which are not only of most relevance to the users' subject interests but which are also the most compatible with their information-seeking habits and method of work.

3. Finding out what is available

The logical progression from the act of assessing the users' needs is to find out what resources are (or soon will be) available. In a well-established service this – at least for printed material – is one aspect of resource selection that is likely to have been taken care of. Over the years a good alerting system is likely to have evolved; certainly most libraries and information units seem to be awash with publishers' catalogues and brochures. Anyone setting up a new service however, or moving into a new subject, will need to develop their own channels of communication to keep informed, using some or all of the following sources:

Promotional literature

The first obvious step is to contact as many relevant publishers as possible, asking to be included on their mailing lists. A useful guide for this purpose is the annual *Writers' and Artists' Yearbook* (A & C Black), which includes a comprehensive list of UK and North American publishers, with a subject breakdown listing their fields of interest. One point to be aware of when browsing through catalogues and brochures is that they are often promoting titles which are still in the preparation stage, many months ahead of publication. Sometimes such works fall by the way-side, either because the author (or editor) is unable to complete the task, or because the demand, as evidenced by the response to the pre-publication details, was insufficient to justify production. In any event ordering too far ahead of publication is not really advisable for budgetary reasons – the prices quoted are usually only approximate, and the actual cost may be considerably higher than expected.

The Bookseller

For general interest material one of the most popular ways of keeping up to date is to scan the weekly issues of *The Bookseller*. As the self-named 'organ of the booktrade' it provides very readable coverage of developments in the area, written not from the angle of librarians but from the viewpoint of publishers and booksellers. Its advertisements are a good source of information on forthcoming titles – this is the place for instance to find out what high profile biographies are due out in the next few months. The subject listings of new books carry much less detail – only the author, title, publisher, edition, price and ISBN. Although this is enough detail for ordering purposes, it is not usually a sufficent basis for selection unless the title is already known, such as a new edition of a popular work or a student (ie cheaper) version of an expensive textbook.

Suppliers' lists

Another current source of information are new title lists, produced by library suppliers such as JMLS (P.O. Box 17, Gamble Street, Nottingham). Both general and profiled lists – tailored to specific subject areas – are normally part of the services which these organisations provide for their customers.

The British National Bibliography (BNB)

More information about the content of publications can be found in *BNB*, the weekly printed issues still widely used for book selection in public and academic libraries. Where *BNB* scores is in its very wide coverage of British material and its detailed records – knowing how many pages there are, whether there is a bibliography and index and if the book is part of a reputable series all help in assessing the value of the work. On the minus side it has to be noted that there can sometimes be delays in the appearance of items; additionally *BNB* excludes specific categories of material – maps, music, and of course material not published or distributed in the UK.

Subject magazines and journals

It is worth keeping an eye on the relevant subject periodicals such as the *New Scientist* and specialist titles within the field of interest. These subject-based journals are one of the best places to pick up details of free publications, such as reports produced by government departments, professional organisations and quangos, which will not be covered by *The Bookseller* or suppliers' lists.

Reference works

For details of existing reference sources, the best place to start is with the magnum opus of British bibliographies, Walford's *Guide to Reference Material*, published in three volumes by the Library Association. Its US counterpart, *Guide to Reference Books* – often referred to as 'Winchell' or 'Sheehy' after two former editors – is published by the American Library Association. Although expensive, both guides now cover printed and electronic sources, backed up by detailed outlines of their contents.

Database information

For commercially produced databases, information is usually readily available from both the publishers or information providers themselves and from the on-line hosts and CD-ROM suppliers. The latter are well-served by the *CD-ROM Directory,* published by TFPL. If funds do not run to the purchase of a directory there is also the CD-ROM catalogue – clear, well-presented and free – distributed by Microinfo (PO Box 3, Omega Park, Alton, Hants, GU34 2PG), one of the largest suppliers in the UK.

Professional literature

One of the best ways of keeping track of electronic resources is by scanning titles such as *Managing Information, Information World Review, Program, Online Review, Online and CD-ROM Review,* and *Electronic Library.* All these include press releases, advertisements and editorial items about new databases, and methods of access. Equally usefully most also carry information on changes to the software or content of existing databases.

Exhibitions and trade fairs

The advantage of these events is that they give the opportunity to view potential resources at first hand, albeit publishers and database producers will be wanting to present their products in the best light possible. Currently the major shows in the UK include the London International Book Fair held in March every year, and the Online Exhibition, also held annually in London in December. The Library Resources Exhibition, which takes place in early June in Birmingham, is also worth a visit although it is equipment, rather than information sources, which tend to predominate.

The combined output of these different sources is likely to be high initially, because of the natural instinct when starting out to cast the net as wide as possible. With time and experience though, it becomes much easier to sift out the 'possibilities' from the 'also rans'.

Internet

In addition to its use as a means of sending and receiving electronic mail, and for telnetting – connecting to host computer services such as Dialog – the Internet can provide access to an enormous range of information, much of which is free. This includes:

- electronic versions of classic, out of copyright books, via Project Gutenberg
- electronic editions of periodicals and newspapers such as The Times and The Guardian
- online journals never published in print
- thousands of databases – everything from skydiving to human rights.

- Selected government information, for example the latest press releases from the Department of Trade and Industry
- catalogues from companies as diverse as Motorola and Benneton
- general interest sources, such as the weather forecasting service from the Meteorological Office.

However as many people are by now aware, one of the big problems with the Internet is the actual location of information. There is no overall system of organisation – finding a relevant resource is often achieved either by luck, considerable perseverance or prior knowledge. The situation is improving – there are an increasing number of search facilities which can be used to access information on the network itself. Broadly speaking these facilities fall into two main groups – networked search tools and subject collections – most of which can be used free of charge.

Networked Search Tools

These tools are actually programs which can be used to automatically search for resources on the Internet. Several of these tools, such as *ARCHIE* and *Veronica* pre-date the World Wide Web (WWW) and have been used in the main by computing and IT enthusiasts. For WWW resources the main route of access to these tools is by means of a software package known as a graphical browser – two of the best-known being Netscape and Mosaic – plus an Internet connection. The WWW tools themselves – often called robots, worms or spiders – operate mainly by wandering about the Internet hunting for new documents. Some index the words in the title and the Uniform Resource Locator (URL), the WWW site or 'address' of the document. Others catalogue all or part of the document itself. When a keyword is typed in it is matched with the index terms. Two of the largest and best known are *Lycos* and *AltaVista*. When trying out these search tools one point to remember is that they are based purely on automatic indexing techniques – as such there will be a large number of false drops. In addition many of these tools can prove slow in use.

Subject collections

These classified guides differ from networked search tools in that they are mostly compiled manually, listing resources selected by volunteers or paid staff. Many take the form of subject trees, with resources grouped under broad headings such as education or history. Under each subject heading are listed sub-groupings, leading on to specific documents; with some subject collections, such as *Yahoo*, this hierarchical approach is augmented by a keyword search facility. Being manually compiled, subject collections are inevitably less up to date, but they are also less likely to retrieve junk since the information has been through some kind of screening process. However most of the popular subject collections are American in origin, and aimed not at the practising librarian or information professional but at the general public.

Library-Orientated Services

In the UK however *BUBL* (originally the **Bu**lletin **B**oard for **L**ibraries) has developed its own subject tree to a range of Internet services and resources, with the support of JISC – the Joint Information Systems Committee of the Higher Education Funding Councils. The *BUBL* Subject Tree can be accessed either alphabetically or via a UDC number. Following the alphabetical 'branch' of the tree leads to major subject headings, which in turn link to specific resources.

Together with the Economic and Social Science Research Council (ESRC), JISC have also funded the development of *SOSIG* – the Social Science Information Gateway. *SOSIG's* function is to collect and organise 'quality' social science resources available on Internet. More subject specific gateways including ones for medicine and engineering are also being developed as part of *eLib* – JISC's Electronic Libraries Program. A consortium of public libraries and the United Kingdom Office for Library Networking (UKOLN) have also launched *Project Earl* (Electronic Access to Resources in Libraries). Amongst other facilities *EARL* is providing a WWW server, giving access to a wide range of general and business sources. Details of the URLs of all these sources is given in Section 9.

Printed Sources

In comparison with these electronic tools, printed sources inevitably suffer badly in terms of currency, but they are a good starting point for anyone yet without access, as well as providing a convenient means of quick reference. With such a fast moving area, picking out specific titles has obvious dangers, but hopefully the ones listed below should prove useful as a starting point.

- *The Gale Guide to Internet Databases, 2nd edition*. Detroit: Gale Research, 1996. Detailed descriptions, plus a subject index, to over 2000 'authoritative' databases in the fields of business, education, research and popular culture.
- *The Whole Internet: User's Guide and Catalog, 2nd edition*. O'Reilly, 1996. Less comprehensive but cheaper, this covers a range of subject resources as well as information on how to use the Internet itself.
- *Net User*. Paragon Publishing. A monthly UK magazine with sections covering new Web resources in education and current affairs, as well as more general, populist sites.
- *Inform* (Institute of Information Scientists). Each monthly issue has a section devoted to new Internet resources, listed by subject fields.

Many other periodicals and newspapers now also include information on new WWW resources, for example each week the *Sunday Times* highlights several new popular sites. As more people gain access, so many more search tools and subject gateways will be developed. The best way of keeping up to date is to be vigilant in noting new search facilities and resources, and trying these out to see how far they meet the needs of an individual service.

4. Selection tools

Despite the trend towards access rather than ownership of information, at the present time most resources are still either purchased outright or leased for on site use. In any service there will be some material which is self-selecting – for example a new Delia Smith cookery book in a public library or updates to the Building Regulations in a construction information unit. For such items the question is not whether to buy but rather how many copies are required. With more marginal resources the decisions are not as clear-cut. Therefore, except for low cost material, some way of evaluating resources in advance of purchase is required. Depending on the type of service, and the cost and nature of the resources, one or more of the following techniques should prove useful.

On-approval collections

These are collections of new books put together for selection purposes by library suppliers. Access arrangements depend on the individual suppliers but generally involve either visiting the showroom or more commonly inspecting a collection sent out to a library's own premises. The great advantage of an 'on appro' collection is that resources can be chosen at first hand – nothing can really beat inspecting a book as a way of assessing its content and presentation. Such a collection also provides the opportunity to discuss works with colleagues and gain a collective view – other staff may have already seen a review of a specific title, or notice that there is a new book on a topic which is under-represented in the current stock. However the collections are of limited value for more specialised topics, such as local studies, likely to be better served by nearby bookshops.

Book shop visits

Basically these visits involve personally inspecting and ordering a range of titles from a large general bookseller such as Dillons or specialist supplier such as the Building Bookshop. Like on-approval collections, a book shop visit gives the opportunity for the direct evaluation of new material plus a useful memory jogger to order extra copies of popular titles already in stock. It is important however to clear such a visit with the relevant purchasing or finance section beforehand in case the regulations prohibit direct ordering in this way.

Inspection copies

In the academic sphere publishers will sometimes provide inspection copies of textbooks – though it must be said that these are aimed not at librarians, but lecturers who may be persuaded to recommend the title to their students. Unless the budget is very tight, trying to obtaining individual copies on this basis is too time-consuming to be worthwhile. With a proposed new journal title however it is worth asking for a specimen copy if only to be certain that it is the correct title that is being ordered; most publishers are willing to send these out to genuine enquirers.

Reviews

Traditionally one of the main selection aids have been reviews – in newspapers, library and information science serials and in the journal literature of the subject itself. Well-written reviews are valuable tools. They can provide expert introductions to unfamiliar topics, indicate likely audiences, highlight good features and draw attention to deficiencies – but remember that reviewers are not infallible and their approach may not necessarily coincide with the needs of a specific service. Ultimately their usefulness will depend to a large extent on the speed with which they are published – those written for the weekend newspapers for instance are usually very up-to-date, occasionally even appearing in advance of publication. Such reviews are invaluable for books of general interest and more specialised but topical titles such as those about the Hubble Space Telescope. However reviews published in specialist journals can be slow to appear – sometimes up to a year or more after publication. In practice it is still worth scanning these for two reasons – as a 'mopping-up' operation to ensure that significant material has not been overlooked, and in helping to make a decision in cases where there are doubts about the worth of a specific item. If funds permit, it may be worth subscribing to *Reference Reviews* (MCB University Press); this contains 'reviews of new reference materials prepared by librarians for librarians', and is both informative and easily assimilated.

Inter-Library Loan

While large-scale borrowing of potential purchases is neither economic or practical, ILL can be useful – for example in a research service when a member of staff asks for an expensive book of questionable value to anyone else. Borrowing the item is sometimes sufficient to satisfy the request. Unless the book is very new or very popular, ILL is often a much quicker way of supplying the item.

Exhibitions and visits

With electronic sources, particularly the more expensive CD-ROMs, previewing before purchase is highly recommended, if not essential. Viewing a source at an exhibition is an effective way of getting an initial 'feel' for a database, although it can be hard to concentrate with a sales executive at your elbow. Where feasible it is worth arranging for an on-site demonstration, giving the opportunity for colleagues and interested users to assess the product. If there is time it is a good idea to draw up a list of queries in advance, to get away from the sales pitch. In addition it may be possible to arrange to see the resource in use within another service – a visit should give the opportunity to find out if the users like the product and whether it is easy to use in practice. It also provides the opportunity to talk about any problems that have arisen and find out how much training and technical support is likely to be needed.

Free trial periods

A further option for CD-ROM is to make use of the free trial period, which suppliers frequently offer for their more expensive subscription-based discs, such as indexes or newspapers. In theory a free trial is a good idea, providing an opportunity for an extended period of assessment by both staff and users. In practice there can be pitfalls – users may be very enthusiastic about the database, especially if it is one of the first CD-ROMs to be acquired in their subject area. If the library staff assessment differs, and the disc is returned then protests can be expected. Where practicable it may be better to set up a trial involving several discs. The evaluation will involve more work but the results are likely to be more objective.

Beta-testing

Occasionally the opportunity to evaluate a new resource may arise during β-testing, the stage at which a new product is assessed by 'real users' before being launched commercially by its publishers. β-testing provides the chance to evaluate a resource exhaustively but free of charge. However it is time-consuming, and requires a positive commitment by the staff involved, who need to keep detailed records of all the problems and queries that arise.

Sometimes none of these selection devices will be either available or appropriate – on approvals collections for instance are usually of too general an interest to be of much use in many special or academic libraries where much book buying is carried out from publishers' catalogues. This promotional literature obviously needs to be viewed with a certain degree of cynicism and carefully scanned – avoiding the creative writing – to see how far the work meets the library's criteria in terms of coverage, level, quality, currency and of course cost.

5. Evaluating the content

Evaluation plays a critical role in the selection process. In essence it involves answering the question 'Is this resource worth buying for my service?' It might seem to newcomers that old hands are able to make instinctive judgements without much effort; in fact such assessments will be based on a set of implicit criteria involving the evaluation of content, relevance, usefulness and the cost of the resource. Drawing up a list of key criteria is useful as an aide memoir, helping to ensure that selection decisions are made on an objective a basis as possible. In the first flush of enthusiasm for a new database for example it is easy to forget to consider whether there are any other better alternatives. Of course not all criteria are relevant to every resource – while much emphasis would rightly be placed on the validation and accuracy of the information in a compendium of engineering data, the decision to buy a CD-ROM of market intelligence reports could be just as concerned with the scope and currency of the database. It is also worth bearing in mind that the old adage, 'Two heads are better than one' applies to resource selection. Talking through a decision with a colleague is the one of the best ways of clarifying the strong and weak points of a product.

Coverage

The obvious place to start is by looking at the scope of the information – the subject field, the type of data, its comprehensiveness and emphasis - to answer basic questions such as:

How broad (or narrow) is the subject coverage?
The remit of many publications is often much wider than could be assumed from their titles. Who would guess from the title for instance that *ERIC* contains abstracts from librarianship journals? However while extended coverage appears to offer 'added value', it must be remembered that marginal topics will be treated in less depth and with more selectivity than the mainstream areas; *ERIC* may not be the best place to look for references on the Follett Report on university libraries. While a general trade directory is a useful first resort for product queries, a narrower, more focused source may be better for finding details of a specific range of machinery.

What type of information is included?

This may seem an unnecessary question but there are now many databases which contain a mix of both bibliographic and full-text information – for example a medical source providing references on health care, complete articles from journals such as *The Lancet* plus material from specialist dictionaries and drug compendia. The type of information tends to have a great effect on the usage of the resource – full-text and numeric databases are enormously popular with users because these provide a 'one-stop', immediate supply of information. However care is needed with the definition of the term 'full-text' – it may mean the selective coverage of items from a range of journals, or the 'cover to cover' inclusion of articles from specified titles.

If the resource is in electronic format, does it include any illustrations, video or sound? If so, how effective are these?

The advent of multi-media has given a tremendous boost to the use of graphics, now becoming a standard feature of many CD-ROMs. Undoubtedly users are attracted by high quality multimedia and, although expensive to produce, good illustrations are a very effective aid to understanding difficult material. The downside is producing a hard copy – firstly it is not always possible to print off the graphics and secondly the prohibitive cost of colour printing means that reproduction is limited to the shades of black, grey and white. While the use of sound, adds to the interest of the material, it may cause problems in quiet environments. The sound may in fact turn out to be an 'optional extra' for some multimedia, such as a CD-ROM on mammalian biology for example where animal noises, though adding to the authenticity, are not vital to the use of the disc. Where the sound is important, it is worth remembering that the workstation must be equipped with an audio-card, not usually included as standard on many machines.

To what extent is the resource comprehensive within its subject field or area of application?

This is an important question to ask, but a much harder one to answer. Publishers and database producers might use phrases such as 'comprehensive bibliographic coverage' or 'a complete overview' but these claims may not be borne out in practice. The first issue is to look at the guidelines used to select information for inclusion – whether the decision is determined by relevancy, by form of material, or some other less obvious criterion. With some trade directories for instance the policy will be to include data on as many relevant companies as possible; others will restrict coverage or give priority in the display only to those organisations paying for their listings. For bibliographic databases the scope will depend partly on the number of journals scanned, and partly on the depth of coverage of each title. While journals on the fringes of the discipline may only be selectively indexed, all papers from the core titles should be included in full. With other types of resource the question is less to do with whether all the relevant information has been included – this would be an impossible task for an encyclopaedia or handbook – but whether the relevant subject fields have been covered to a sufficient depth. Here the information needs to be neither too cursory nor too complex, not an easy balance to achieve.

Are there any obvious omissions?

Just as significant as knowing what has been included, is assessing what has been left out. Inevitably there will be omissions - every publication or database has its limits, but the deliberate exclusions should be apparent from the selection criteria. It is the inconsistencies which cause the most irritation – a bibliographic database which does not include one of the major journals in the field, or a professional directory that excludes major names because the people concerned did not return their questionnaires. Some exclusions may be the result of copyright or licensing restrictions – a full-text CD-ROM for instance which does not include the publications of a major organisation because an agreement could not be reached between the owners of the information and the publishers of the database.

A general issue which also needs to be considered is whether the coverage is slanted in any way. Many of the encyclopaedias and other educational materials published on CD-ROM are written from the American point of view. Although otherwise of good quality, this emphasis tends to detracts from their use – for example the first version of *Encarta*, Microsoft's best-selling encyclopaedia, included extensive coverage of American sports, but made hardly any mention of popular British games such as rugby and cricket. Traditionally the coverage of many American abstracts and indexes has been biased towards US titles, with only the major British journals being included. Some of the newer electronic document delivery services also share a geographical slant; ADONIS, the biomedical database mentioned earlier, was launched by a consortium of European publishers, a fact still reflected to a large extent in its journal coverage. Of course a bias in coverage can be turned to account – many of the newest theories and practices in the management field for example originate in the US – but it is best recognised at the selection stage, not when the resource is in stock.

Level

There are some standard well-established reference works which appeal to a very wide audience – for example it would probably be impossible to categorise the users of the *Guinness Book of Records*. For other material though, it is as well to clarify the relevance of the information by asking the sort of questions below:

Who is the publication aimed at – children, the public at large or commercial and academic environments?

If it is to meet the needs of the target audience, the information must be conveyed at the appropriate level – for example while a handbook on electrical engineering would be a good source of information on power transmission, a student wanting diagrams on how to wire plugs and sockets would need a more basic source. This need to provide information at the right level is especially the case for school libraries, catering for the needs of children and young teenagers. Although CD-ROMs have proved very successful in this environment, many databases that are understandable by the educated layperson or undergraduate, can be way over the heads of the pupils, even those at the top end of secondary education. Particularly with scientific and technical sources there is likely to be a distinction between those with a factual emphasis and those that take a critical evaluative approach. This practical emphasis is not just limited to handbooks – the choice of journals for full-text databases on CD-ROM may well be determined by the need for product-specific data and company information.

Matching the appropriate level to the users' needs can require a broad view on occasions. Some children's books, such as Simon and Schuster's *Country Fact Files* series, in practice often prove to be useful for adults needing to check basic facts or wanting background information.

Currency

High up on the list of criteria for assessing any resource is its currency. No one wants to use out of date information, and electronic publication has meant that we now have far higher expectations in terms of timeliness. Initial points to consider are:

How up to date is the information?

Everyone probably has their own private list of material which is out of date even at the time of purchase, such as a directory in which it seems that half the companies have gone into receivership, but for some types of resource currency is vital. With CAS-IAS services such as *UnCover* for instance, not only is it important that as wide a range of journals as possible is included but also that the most recent issues are listed.

Will the information be revised on a continuous basis?

It is not just electronic material which is updated at frequent intervals; printed reference sources are also revised by a variety of means, from the amendment slips issued by the British Standards Institution to the loose-leaf sheets beloved of legal publishers. With these revisions comes an on-going financial commitment – often in the order of several hundred pounds a year – quite apart from the amount of staff time which is required to file them.

How frequent are the updates?

Are these issued at regular time intervals or on an ad hoc basis? The updates to abstracts and indexes, whether on-line, CD-ROM or hard copy should be published according to regular time schedules, but with other types of resource the frequency of revision is not always as clear cut. In areas such as surveying and construction, there are handbooks which are updated at irregular time intervals, depending on when there have been sufficient or important enough changes to warrant publishing a revision. Though a plus from the currency point of view, it is important to be aware of such revisions to ensure that the LIS arranges (and budgets) to receive these regularly.

Whether a very high degree of currency matters of course, is really dependent on the needs of the users – as witnessed by the growth of CD-ROM. One of the biggest problems of this medium is its lack of current information, but this has not prevented it being a roaring success in academic libraries, where timeliness though important is normally subservient to cost. It is significant that one of the areas in which CD-ROM has made less headway is the business and financial sector, where the timeliness of the data is vital.

Quality

Traditionally the evaluation of printed reference tools has placed great emphasis on the authority, accuracy and presentation of the material. This concern with quality is equally valid for electronic sources, particularly with the development of the Internet. Some concerns to bear in mind include:

How good is the physical quality and content of the resource?

For printed material the standard of presentation – the paper, the binding and the way the information is presented – is important. One of the main reasons for the success of the Dorling Kindersley titles such as the *Eyewitness* books is the attractiveness of the graphics and the way these are interlinked with the text.

What is the standing of the publisher or database producer?

At issue here is the credibility of the 'owner' of the information, whether this be a commercial organisation, professional society or academic body. Though not infallible, it is reasonable to expect a certain level of authority and accuracy from well-established publishers, institutions, and universities, who have their reputations to protect.

Is the information subject to any kind of review?

Refereeing procedures have long been used by printed journals as a way of filtering out inaccurate, spurious or unsuitable papers. Some form of peer review is also an important consideration for resources such as encyclopaedias, handbooks and data compilations. One indication that the publication has been subject to validation is the presence of an editorial or advisory board, whose members have recognisable, reputable affiliations – they guide the content and choice of contributors, who should also be experts in their fields.

The situation regarding the quality of information accessed via the Internet is much more complicated, as witnessed by the growing public concern over some of the material now available. Basically it is possible to 'publish' almost anything – the individual or organisation creating the site obviously controls the information which appears. If the data is needed for serious purposes, it pays to proceed with some caution, checking the information for its authenticity and currency. Once the novelty of the Internet has worn off there is likely to be much more concern over the quality of the information available. It is significant that SOSIG and the other subject collections established by the *eLib* program have adopted a policy of filtering out any information that is out of date, inappropriate, local in content, no longer available or of little use.

Indexing

With the current emphasis on computerised access to information, it is easy to overlook the value of good indexing of material. For printed resources though, the question of how well the information has been indexed is still very important. A handbook or encyclopaedia which has been poorly indexed or arranged is going to be less cost- effective, apart from being the cause of much frustration. For information in electronic format the quality of the indexing is equally relevant, although the search software and user interface are also vital components of the retrieval process. Some points to consider include:

What indexes are supplied (and in what format)?

Unless the information is arranged alphabetically by subject, it is reasonable to expect printed reference works to include subject (and where appropriate) author indexes. Specialised indexes may be appropriate for some publications, such as an alpha-numeric list by part number in an electronic components directory. It is also no longer safe to assume that the indexes will appear in the same format as the main work – a few scientific and technical books for example are now supplied (and sold) separately on floppy disk. If this is so, a computer will need to be made available and arrangements for accessing the indexes will be required.

Are controlled terms used?

The old dispute between the use of free and controlled vocabulary for abstracts and indexes gets less of a hearing nowadays, with computerised searching becoming so commonplace. It is true that users tend to prefer the natural language approach – usually through the lack of knowledge of anything better – but controlled vocabulary is still a very useful tool in the hands of the library staff. Users searching CD-ROM databases such as *ABI* or *Medline* can often be found scanning through hundreds of references at a time; once the purpose of the descriptors has been explained though, it is nearly always possible to help them narrow down their results to a more relevant, manageable quantity.

How accurate and consistent is the indexing?

Without 'hands-on' experience this question is obviously difficult to answer, but enough has been published to suggest that many bibliographic databases are inadequate in this respect. A recent investigation of database quality found several such examples, including a major index in which the subject heading 'CD – ROM' was sometimes spelled both with and without the spaces, a mistake which would have resulted in 40% of references being lost.

One indicator of the growing interest in this area is the establishment by the Library Association and United Kingdom On-line User Group of the Centre for Information Quality Management (CIQM) to act as a clearinghouse to which problems with the quality of bibliographic databases can be reported. Such problems include citations to non-existent articles, duplicate records, and in one instance the complete absence of a core journal from a major source after its name had been changed. The most highly rated database to emerge from reports so far is *Inspec*, with the fewest errors and the best access, for both the CD-ROM and on-line versions. CIQM are establishing a 'labelling' system for bibliographic databases, which would cover the number of records, the subject and geographical coverage, plus some kind of quotient or rating to show the depth of the indexing, its consistency and accuracy. The latter indicator would cover aspects such as spelling mistakes, inconsistent hyphenation and typing errors, the cause of so many inaccuracies in database indexes.

Alternatives

With an expensive purchase, it also makes sense to look at what else is available. In terms of the subject coverage this can be boiled down into two questions:

How does the content compare with competitor products (print or electronic)?

It may be that the information perfectly fills a gap in the market, but most resources are not unique, and it is likely that there will be some overlap with existing material. The demarcation lines between most bibliographic databases have always been blurred and many newer resources similarly exhibit considerable overlap. The human body for example is proving to be a very popular target for multi-media CD-ROMs, with a host of discs now being marketed on anatomy and physiology, seemingly varying to the untutored eye only in the level of the graphics, video and sound provided.

Is there anything else already available in stock or accessible via a network which could meet the need?

With the continuing squeeze on funding, the phrase 'already available' may need to be interpreted liberally – for printed sources, which are not subject to the licensing conditions normally applied to databases, this could mean limited use of other local collections, though 'free-loading' – referring to resources without any prior agreements – must be avoided. If nothing else, assessing a potential purchase against information already in stock may show up where changes could be made, such as the cancellation of older subscriptions or standing orders and the discarding of obsolete material.

Cost

As with so many other aspects of the selection process, establishing the cost is not always as straightforward as it may seem. While the cost of a printed publication such as a single volume directory or handbook is normally self-evident, many other resources are no longer purchased outright at a clearly stated price. For electronic information the pricing structure can be quite complex, especially if the data is to be leased rather than purchased outright. Network licenses and discounting arrangements are discussed in detail in Section 8, the issues raised here being concerned with the initial cost of buying a resource.

What does the price include?

The first point to clarify is exactly what is being supplied. Many large bibliographic and full-text databases are marketed both as complete files and as sub-sets – all British Standards for example are now available on CD-ROM, both as a complete service and in twelve separate sections covering areas such as health and safety, and domestic, office and institutional equipment. Obviously a sub-set of a large database will be cheaper, but it is important to be sure that the field covered is central to the users' interests. Sub-sets are unlikely to be of value for a service that needs to take a wide view of a subject, because there is a real risk of missing relevant information. However if currency is not absolutely critical, money can sometimes be saved by opting for more infrequent updates to databases – subscribing to the quarterly rather than the monthly version of a CD-ROM for example may cut the cost by several hundred pounds a year.

Are there any hidden charges?

It is worth investigating whether there are any extra costs not obvious at first glance. Subscribers to the printed journals of a large publisher for instance were at one stage automatically supplied with disc versions of the periodicals – but at an additional, compulsory charge. With most databases on CD-ROM or diskette, the price is usually quoted exclusive of VAT (Value Added Tax), although this is payable at the rate of 17.5%.

Are any additional services included?

On the brighter side it could be that additional facilities or services are included in the price. For example Technical Indexes, the company marketing British Standards on CD-ROM, supports this with a free enquiry service to their customers, while the Royal Institution of Chartered Surveyors offer subscribers to the *RICS Abstracts and Reviews* an enquiry service, which includes limited searching of their in-house database plus photocopying and loan of materials from their Library.

Like buying a car, with resources where the costs runs into thousands the stated price may only be the starting point. Sales executives often have some degree of flexibility over the cost and timing of a purchase, especially if the company are selling several of their products to the same organisation. It may not come naturally to many librarians but the ability to negotiate can be a very useful asset.

6. Evaluating the software

Selecting electronic resources involves more than just evaluating the content – it is also necessary to assess the quality of the software needed to retrieve and display the information available. While good software cannot improve poor information, there are enough examples of good discs marred by inadequate software to make it worthwhile expending some effort at this stage.

User interface

One of the most important characteristics of any resource in electronic format is the user interface, the software and hardware forming the link between the searcher and the database itself. In practical terms this link is made up of a number of elements – the instructions used to tell the computer to carry out an activity, the keyboard, mouse or other devices used to input these instructions, the way information is displayed on screen, and the facilities provided to help people who need assistance. Evaluating an interface involves assessing how effectively these elements combine to enable fast, easy retrieval of information. If something is difficult to search, slow to respond or unreliable, only the most persistent or enthusiastic users are likely to bother a second or third time. Those who do persevere will take up a lot of staff time, frustrating for all. The main points to consider are:

What IT platforms – the type of operating system and hardware – are available?

For CD-ROM the main choice lies between Windows, MS-DOS and Macintosh although other platforms such as UNIX are becoming more widely used. Graphical User Interfaces (GUIs) such as Windows are popular with 'computer literate' users, who quickly become familiar with the functions available. However people without previous experience are likely to need to time to acclimatise themselves to handling a mouse, opening and closing windows, and pulling down menus. How long DOS-based products will continue to be supported by the publishers is a moot point – SilverPlatter, the largest CD-ROM publisher, are no longer carrying out any development work on their MS-DOS interface, which may come to have an 'old-fashioned' look to it in a few years time.

27

Is the interface user-friendly?

This is one of the key criteria for judging an interface, if a database is intended to be searched by the users themselves. 'User-friendliness' may seem a nebulous concept to assess, since it depends to some extent on subjective judgements. However there are certain design principles which may be useful to follow as a checklist. Firstly the interface should be designed to be as flexible as possible, for ease of use by both beginners and experts. Some DOS-based interfaces such as Knight-Ridder's DIALOG OnDisc offer two search modes – an 'easy menu' and a command option for experienced users. Another way of providing such flexibility is by designing two separate interfaces. The *Financial Times* for instance is available in two versions, Easy Search, a straightforward DOS interface and a more advanced 'freeway' Windows interface. Secondly the interface should enable easy 'navigation' or movement around the database from screen to screen, from one hit to the next, and from one part of a record to another. Without good navigational techniques it can be easy for a user to feel 'lost', particularly with Windows where there is less control than in a DOS-based interface over the sequence of actions. Thirdly it is important that users should not be left wondering what to do next – if an action needs to be carried out it should be indicated on screen, for example by a bar saying 'Click here to see report'. The final point – although it may seem self-evident – is that users should be kept informed while processing is taking place, by a message or symbol, so that they do not think they have been dropped by the system.

Is the screen display clear and well-laid out?

The presentation of information on screen has a major influence on the ease of use. One of the problems of screen displays is clutter. Too much information or poor layout will confuse users. Terminology is also important – users may not understand technical jargon such as 'limit with additional concepts'. Colour too plays a large role in screen displays – not only as a highlighter but also as a means of delineating specific types of information. Actions for example are often displayed in red, with more restful colours such as white and blue for text. The difficulty is that judgements on the use of colour tend to be subjective – what some people find annoying others find perfectly acceptable. Useful guidelines to bear in mind are that generally no more than four colours should be used in any one display, and that the use of colour should be applied consistently across an interface. If red is chosen for instance to indicate an action it should not later be used to highlight text.

How reliable is the interface?

Although it may seem an obvious point, it is worth stating that the system should function correctly. An interface which freezes in mid search, leaving a puzzled user wondering what is happening, will cause a lot of irritation and frustration. One test is to see what happens if a very common word such as 'education' is input. Does the system stall completely or just carry out the search very slowly?

An interface should also be tolerant of user error – it should not crash for example if a user attempts to download information onto an unformatted disc. An 'Exit/ Abandon' option should also be displayed on screen at all times to enable the user to recover from such mistakes.

Is there adequate 'user assistance'?

No matter how effective a system, good support facilities are also needed. The on-screen help should be context sensitive, so that a user wanting to find out how to print off data does not have to wade through a display of information about searching techniques first. There should be meaningful error messages too, not displaying a phrase such as 'Improper search syntax' for instance when a query is input using upper rather than lower case. Good printed documentation is also a real asset to the LIS staff, and one area in which CD-ROM publishers often fall down. Some publishers do not produce a printed manual at all, relying only on 'read me' files on installation software. However there are also some good examples. One of the best is the manual accompanying the financial database FAME, which explains in clear understandable style how to carry out complex comparisons of numerical data from company accounts.

With the huge growth in the CD-ROM market there is now a bewildering array of interfaces available – a confusing situation for staff and users alike. Only where the databases are supplied by the same publisher such as SilverPlatter or Knight-Ridder will there be any uniformity. One factor to consider therefore when adding to an existing collection of CD-ROMs is whether there are already discs in stock which use the same interface – if so buying another product from the same 'stable' can ease the problems of training and familiarisation for both users and staff. In the future it is likely that more and more electronic resources will also become available with a Web interface – a move which will introduce an element of 'standardisation' in this area.

Searching and output facilities

Along with a reliable, user-friendly interface, an electronic resource needs good fast searching facilities, if it is to be cost-effective. After more than two decades of developments in computerised information retrieval, it is easy to assume that adequate, if not exceptional, searching capabilities will be provided. However it is wise to check how well these work, by looking at the following points.

What is the main search mode?

It may not always seem apparent but for bibliographic and full-text databases there are two main search modes: browse and keyword. The first mode leads a user into an alphabetical display of indexed words, from which the most appropriate one(s) for the topic can be selected. In keyword search mode there is no display of words – the system looks for a term exactly as it is input. Browse mode tends to be easier to use, especially where the topic can be described with a single keyword. The system helps the user to make the right choice of spelling and word-ending, but does not offer much scope for more complex topics. In keyword searching it should be possible to combine two or more terms to state more precisely what information is required, but it allows more scope for error. If the keywords are spelt wrongly or combined together incorrectly then nothing will be retrieved even though information is present in the database. Although most systems provide both search modes, the layout and presentation of the options on screen is likely to ensure that one will be more obvious than the other – and this by default will be the one most users will choose.

Are all the standard search capabilities available?

These capabilities include the use of the Boolean operators AND, OR and NOT to combine keywords together, and a truncation facility to search for the variant endings of word-stems. Some search software also provides for the automatic retrieval of the singular and plural versions of a word. The ability to carry out a word proximity search for terms adjacent to each other is essential in a full text database otherwise too much irrelevant information will be retrieved. Field limitation – the facility to restrict the search to a specific part of a record – is also important. In a database such as the *Guardian* or *Times* on CD-ROM for example one of the main ways of cutting down the information obtained to a manageable size is to search only for keywords in the titles of articles.

What additional features are present?

For bibliographic databases such as *ERIC* an on-line version of the thesaurus can be valuable, since it minimises the hit and miss approach of scanning through the references retrieved to find relevant subject descriptors or indexing words. Although not that common, lateral searching – a facility enabling users to scan through a set of retrieved records to select a new keyword, and then instruct the system to carry out a search for this term – is useful since it saves people the time and effort of inputting it themselves. With bibliographic databases too, the facility to 'flag' citations to journals available on-site can also be a useful feature.

How fast is the response time – the number of seconds between initiating a search (or other action) and the displaying of the results?

There is evidence to suggest that this should be no more than about 15 seconds – any longer is likely to lead to errors and irritation. Although the search software obviously has a major influence on performance however, it is not the only factor. With CD-ROMs the speed and power of the hardware is also very important – the response time can usually be improved dramatically by using a workstation with a faster processor, larger hard disc and high speed drive unit.

How is the output displayed?

With newer software there is the possibility that the results may be ranked in order of relevance, so that the most important items are displayed first. Relevance ranking is still the exception rather than the norm though – most software used to search bibliographic and full-text databases show the results shown by date, usually in reverse chronological order so that the latest information is seen first. However there a few databases around in which the oldest record is displayed first, a frustrating situation if a lot of information has been retrieved.

What printing and downloading facilities are available?

It is reasonable to expect to be able to download as well as print off information retrieved during a search. Most times this assumption is correct but there are exceptions – it is not normally possible for instance to download from CD-ROMs such as the British Standards on disc, because the information is stored in the form of facsimile images, not as ASCII text.

Can the software be customised to control the level of output?

Libraries frequently need to be able to restrict the amount of printing carried out to prevent the workstations being monopolised by a few users; software which can be customised to enable limits to be set locally has clear attractions in such circumstances. Variable display and printing formats – as provided by many bibliographic databases – are also very useful, enabling the most appropriate layout for an individual service to be selected as the default setting.

Although less common than a few years ago, there may be occasions when the same database is available from different suppliers – a prime example of this is *Medline*, available on CD-ROM from several alternative sources – raising the question of which version to purchase. In these circumstances a number of factors will need to assessed – not just the user interface, and the search and output facilities, but also the length of the back files available, the number of years of data on each disk and of course the cost.

7. Delivery mechanisms

Knowing what the users' needs are and what information is available is essential, but on its own is not sufficient. To apply the knowledge to best practical effect, it must be linked as closely as possible to the overall level of resourcing – not just the funding for new material, vital though this is, but also to the computing facilities available and the staffing levels in operation. In the past selection was relatively simple – generally speaking libraries bought as much as possible and kept it indefinitely. Now with so much information produced and sold in electronic format all this has changed. Currently there is much discussion about the move from a holdings to an access strategy in libraries. Although sometimes presented as an either/or scenario, the two approaches can be complementary – purchasing or flat rate subscriptions for resources likely to be in heavy demand, 'pay-as-you-go' use for information needed on a less frequent or one-off basis. Essentially this policy can be summed up in the quotation: 'Buy the core, access the rest, and be quick about it!'

Options

Buying the core and accessing the rest though, now requires a reasonable awareness of what delivery mechanisms are available. For some information in electronic format, the choice can be confusingly wide. The main options are:

Stand-Alone CD-ROM

Now established as a relatively mature technology, CD-ROM offers not one but several mechanisms for the delivery of information. The simplest is still the stand-alone workstation – a computer, one or more CD-ROM drives, plus an optional printer. This type of system can work well for resources likely to receive a reasonable amount of use and in one location only. The costs are fixed and pre-determined, making budgeting much easier than with on-line systems. The speed, ease of use and retrieval capabilities of CD-ROM are a great improvement on some print-based counterparts. Where there is a high level of demand though, the single-user facility can become a bottle-neck, restricting access to the information.

Networked CD-ROM

Developed to overcome the physical barrier of single access, networked systems come in a variety of configurations or forms, ranging from those linking several workstations in one building to those serving hundreds of users across a large campus. In terms of the usage of resources, networking has two significant advantages – it enables simultaneous searching by a number of people and it allows remote access from workstations sited away from the location of the discs themselves. However taking a decision to invest in a CD-ROM network involves balancing the benefits of improved access against the expense and possibility of technological obsolescence, an assessment outside the scope of this work. If a network is already installed, the obvious practical course of action is to consider adding new resources, provided that this is technically feasible, permitted under the licensing conditions and that the costs are not prohibitive.

Locally-Mounted Databases

Another option is to load databases on to an in-house computer system, by transferring information distributed on CD-ROM, magnetic tape, or diskette. Workstations connected to a local area network can then access the information directly from the library's computer system, speeding up the searching time considerably. However it is imperative to clear this arrangement with the publisher concerned to avoid infringing copyright.

Client-Server Access to CD-ROMs

A recent initiative has been the development by Silver Platter of ERL (Electronic Reference Library) technology. With this technology the workload is divided between the user's workstation, running the retrieval software (the client), and the computer system (server) hosting the CD-ROM databases and search software. This approach has the advantage of maximising the use of the network, and enables fast, easy access using a choice of interfaces and a range of IT platforms.

On-line Access via Commercial Hosts

While CD-ROM works well in environments where self-service is a viable option, it has two drawbacks – its lack of currency and expense. With fixed, pre-determined charges, the fewer the users the higher the cost of each search. Commercial on-line hosts such as Dialog have long been used as a way of meeting the need for a wide range of resources, but at a low level of demand. On-line databases are also vital where users need current information – CD-ROM cannot compare in terms of currency. In an effort to attract end-users many hosts have introduced simpler interfaces though charging mechanisms are still mostly based on a 'pay-as-you-use' rather than subscription basis, not likely to encourage librarians to let users have a free hand.

33

FIRSTSEARCH

One notable exception is FIRSTSEARCH – an end-user on-line service hosted by OCLC. In a radical move OCLC have eliminated connect-time and record-display charges – users are able to choose between paying an annual flat rate subscription or pre-search pricing. With the latter option, blocks of searches are bought in advance, the larger the number purchased, the cheaper the search. This simple pricing structure, wide range of popular databases, and user-friendly interface is making FIRSTSEARCH an attractive proposition to many libraries.

On-line Access via Academic Networking

Under the impetus of JISC, a selection of databases – mainly bibliographic resources – has been established for higher education institutions in the UK. Most of the databases are loaded at the BIDS data centre at Bath University, staff and students logging in via JANET (Joint Academic Network) directly from their own workstations. The costs are met by their parent institutions who are charged an annual fee for each database to which they choose to subscribe. Although the range of databases on offer is not large, those available are mostly major services chosen for their wide appeal. This type of on-line access has proved very popular with academics for the following reasons – an easy-to-use interface, popular databases, current information, and convenient 'free' access. To make a subscription viable however there must be sufficient interest either from the institution as a whole or from specific departments, and enough users with their own workstations.

On-line Access Directly to Publishers

Gradually more publishers are providing direct access to their databases, eliminating the need for a host as a 'middleman'. Some of these are bibliographic and full-text databases, accessed via a modem and 'dial-up' telecommunications link, and with pricing mechanisms ranging from a flat rate annual subscription, pre-paid purchase of a certain number of hours of searching time, or the more 'conventional' arrangement of retrospective billing per minute of connect time. A rapidly growing number of journals though can now be accessed directly over the Internet. In such journals the likelihood is that the papers would be 'published' at least a few days in advance of the print version. With these electronic editions, links may be provided between the original article, and any letters, retractions or editorials on the same subject. With printed copies of course it is necessary to search physically through subsequent issues to find these contributions. Connections to other related sources of information are also feasible, such as a direct link between the citations at the end of an article and a bibliographic database. Selecting a specific citation will then bring up the full reference on screen, including an abstract and full details of the author's affiliation, to help the user decide whether it is worth obtaining a copy of the paper.

With all the publicity about electronic access however, it is easy to overlook the fact that the two most common delivery mechanisms are still hard-copy and inter-library loan – over 3.5 million requests were made to the British Library's Document Supply Centre (DSC) for instance during 1993/94; a situation likely to continue for some time to come.

Method of supply

Deciding on the best mechanism of supply for a specific resource means assessing all the feasible options – whether paper-based or electronic – in the light of the users' needs and the available funding. In some cases the choice between the alternative methods of supply is simple – a request for an article from an obscure conference for instance is clearly best satisfied by obtaining a photocopy from the DSC. For other resources the answers are not so clear cut. The selection of the most appropriate resource and delivery mechanism depends on the combination of a number of factors involving not just the choice of the most relevant, cost effective publications or databases available on the market but also wider issues such as the hardware and software requirements, technical feasibility, and policy issues such as space and staffing considerations.

Format

One issue which arises more and more nowadays is the choice of format. When an established reference work such as the *Aslib Directory of Information Sources in the United Kingdom* for example becomes available on CD-ROM, which is the more appropriate version to buy? Is it better to go for the improved searching facilities of CD-ROM or stay with the convenience of print? The first issue to clarify are the differences – if any – between the alternative versions. The tendency is to expect the computerised version of a resource to contain at least as much if not more information than its printed counterpart . With the current awareness service *Current Contents* for instance the CD-ROM version includes the author abstracts, not available in the printed edition. However it is not safe to assume this will always be true – the disc versions of newspapers such as *The Times*, *Guardian* or *Independent* include hardly any of the photographs or diagrams that appear in the daily printed copies. More often than not the price of the CD-ROM is higher than the print version, but again there can be a few surprises. The disc version of *Encyclopaedia Britannica* for instance would appear to be a bargain here, since it has been marketed at one third less than the price of the print volumes. However it is important to be clear what is on offer. Although a directory on CD-ROM may be more expensive, it is often the case that the electronic version will be updated more frequently. This price could well include a six monthly update disc, whereas the hard copy price would be for one annual volume only.

Convenience

A second point to consider is what is the most convenient option, both in terms of retrieving the information and physical access to the resource. Where there is a choice between the print or electronic version of a directory for instance, the computerised version will have obvious benefits in terms of searching – faster access, more ways of searching the data and the facility to print off or download the records founds. Against this has to be weighed the fact that it is usually easier to scan information in print, and to 'look around' an entry to see what else is relevant. There is also a marked difference between resources used for quick reference and those needed for lengthy periods of study. With a directory on CD-ROM for instance it may take more time and effort to fetch the disc, load it on to a workstation, and then carry out the search than it would to take a single volume off the shelves in the reference area and scan the data manually. On the other hand if the information is likely to be heavily used and can be permanently loaded on a convenient computer, or if mailing addresses need to be printed off, buying the disc may be the best solution.

Level of use

The likely level of use of a resource is another aspect of provision which must be assessed, as this will have huge bearing on the means of supply. Take for example a fairly typical scenario of an industrial or academic library trying to meet the needs of its users to keep up to date with an important but expensive journal. With limited funding, is this requirement best satisfied by buying the title, borrowing copies from the British Library, accessing the electronic edition (if available), or making use of *UnCover* or one of the other CAS-IAS services now on the market? Attempting to quantify the demand for a new resource is not easy, but it is necessary to try to get some idea even if this is only a very rough estimate. With a new journal subscription for instance, it is important to determine if the title is of interest to most of the members of a department or research group or just one or two people. If the latter then the cost per consultation will be high, and if those members of staff subsequently leave the journal will no longer have any relevance. In such a case it would almost certainly be cheaper to take the CAS-IAS route, or to borrow copies on an ad hoc basis – though the fact that there is now a ban preventing the loan of a large number of well-used titles until several months after their publication would need to be taken into account.

Hardware and software requirements

When making a decision to buy or access information in electronic format, the implications in terms of the hardware and telecommunications requirements also need to be thought through carefully. Will new equipment be needed or is the existing kit sufficient? If an electronic encyclopaedia on CD-ROM is being purchased for example, it can probably be used on a workstation already running several discs. On the other hand, a large full text database containing scanned images and requiring dozens of discs to store the information will most likely necessitate the purchase of a new, high specification (and more expensive) computer and a tower CD-ROM unit. A laser printer will also be essential for printing off the information. Even if the database is affordable, the cost of the hardware could well turn out to be prohibitive. Software requirements also need to be taken into account – if for instance a decision is made to access the electronic edition of a journal then the workstation(s) will need to be equipped with the appropriate software so that any photographs and diagrams can be downloaded. The technical feasibility of the delivery mechanism also needs to be considered particularly if planning to network a CD-ROM. As a medium CD-ROM was originally designed for stand-alone use, not multi-access, and there can be technical problems in networking some discs. Before making concrete arrangements to network a specific CD-ROM, it is vital to ensure this is technically feasible.

Ownership and licensing

A very significant factor particularly in the purchase of CD-ROMs is the question of ownership. While one-off products such as *Encarta* are sold outright, many bibliographic and full-text databases on disc are only leased on a subscription basis. Customers do not obtain ownership, only rights of use for a certain period of time. With a very few exceptions, printed material is acquired for permanent retention. Before taking out a subscription to a CD-ROM it is important to clarify the licensing conditions, and whether the principle of 'lapsing ownership' applies, that is whether the discs have to be returned if the database is later cancelled. Some licensing agreements also require either the return or destruction of superseded discs, preventing these being passed on to other service points within an organisation. It is also possible to build metering systems into CD-ROMs, so that the discs 'time-out' after a specified period of use. Warranty provisions for replacing discs need to be considered too, and it is worth asking what the publisher's policy would be if a disc is lost, stolen or damaged. Whatever the licensing conditions or warranty provisions specify, it is never wise to sign an agreement without checking with the service's management.

Staffing requirements

The selection of information resources is not a task which can be carried out in isolation – what information is chosen and how this is used will have a direct impact on other activities, most immediately and obviously on the reference and enquiry service. Nowhere has this been more apparent than in academic libraries where the workload of the reference desk staff has increased dramatically since the advent of CD-ROM. This being so, when a new database is being considered for either access or purchase, it is important to assess what level of help will be needed to use it. If the interface is hard to fathom, will there be sufficient trained staff available on a continual basis to help users with their searches? Good technical back-up is also absolutely essential in the provision of any electronic resource. If there are hardware, software or network problems, can these be dealt with quickly or will the resource be out of action for several days before assistance is obtained? The users will soon lose faith if the difficulties cannot be resolved rapidly.

Effect on other library services and activities

With any changes in information resource provision, it is important to ask what effects there are likely to be on other library stock and services, particularly the ILL and document delivery service. If a subscription to a new bibliographic database is being considered, it is worth bearing in mind that one of the spin-offs will almost certainly be an increase in the number of ILL requests. Although it may not be the deciding factor, it is a good idea to check what proportion of the journals indexed are actually in stock. In public and academic libraries too, the desire to provide easy access unfortunately has to be balanced against the need to keep the information secure. In this respect electronic formats are likely to provide better measures of protection – while the print copy of a journal can be easily vandalised or stolen for instance, the CD-ROM or on-line version will not be subject to the same problem. Space considerations also need to be taken into account. On the whole electronic resources would appear to have the advantage here, though if the physical location is very limited there may be difficulties in finding enough space to locate the hardware

Cost-effectiveness

Ultimately the major consideration must be to choose the most cost-effective solution, bearing in mind not simply the cost of the resource, but also its implications in terms of equipment and support and – just as importantly – the ease and satisfaction of use. Whatever the delivery mechanism selected, it is vital never to lose sight of the needs of the users – they are the ultimate recipients of the information and the means of supply should suit their requirements. With so much emphasis on new technology it is easy to forget that however technically advanced a system, it should still offer something at least as good as if not better than what is already in place. If not the information will not receive much use and the money will have been wasted.

8. Budgeting and other management issues

Budgeting is a central activity in the provision of information – a balancing act between maximising the resources available while staying within the inevitable funding constraints. The issue of cost effectiveness has already been raised in relation to the means of supply. However there are other points which need to considered when budgeting – whether VAT is payable, if a discount can be negotiated, the charges if the resource is networked, and whether there are any recurrent costs.

VAT

Although there has been moves to levy VAT on all printed resources, currently at least books and journals are zero rated in the UK. With other resources the situation is more complicated. While no VAT is payable on printed data which is supplied with free software, CD-ROMs and databases supplied on diskette are liable for the tax at the full rate. Since the prices quoted are usually exclusive of VAT, in practice this means adding 17.5% to the cost of the database. Standard-rate tax is also payable on books of plans and drawings, and on educational texts in a question and answer format, in which spaces are left for the insertion of replies.

Discounts

With information being marketed more and more as a commodity and the changing structure of the book trade, the situation regarding discounts and other special offers is becoming increasingly complicated. As far as books are concerned, with exceptions such as pre-publication offers, few reductions are available for titles ordered directly from a publisher – one reason why acquisitions departments are likely to discourage staff from purchasing on-approval copies. To receive a discount it is necessary to obtain the books from a library supplier or book shop, the level of discount being determined by the type of book and the contract between the supplier and the service. Under the terms of the former Net Book Agreement (NBA) this discount – only available to libraries which permit access to members of the public – could not exceed 10%. With the recent demise of the NBA all this is now changing. Some libraries are demanding much larger discounts; some suppliers on the other hand are saying that profit margins are too narrow to allow a large increase and to continue with additional services provided such as book jacketing and labelling.

For CD-ROMs and more specialised material though, the range of offers can be wide – discounts for the purchase of multiple years of a file, for the renewal of an existing publication, for buying additional copies of a disc, for taking the print as well as the electronic version of a database, and general reductions for educational and non-profit making institutions. The latter can be surprisingly generous – on occasions as much as half the standard price. However a close watch needs to be kept on the time scale, not only for pre-publication discounts, where a closing date is normally specified, but also for other offers arranged directly with a sales executive. Obtaining internal approval and completing the necessary paper-work for a purchase can take some time and it is important to ensure that the offer will be held until clearance has been completed.

Consortia purchasing

Another factor to consider is whether the resource is available through a consortia or co-operative purchasing scheme, via which discounts could be obtained. In the higher education area for instance, CHEST – the Combined Higher Education Software Team – are now well-known for the site licences they have negotiated with certain software and database publishers. These licences enable all the students and staff at an institution to use a product for the cost of a single, fixed annual subscription, usually at a price well below the market value. More recently the Higher Education Funding Council (HEFC) launched an initiative giving universities the option to purchase certain journals at reduced rates. Under the Pilot Site Licence Scheme for Libraries, the HEFC are making lump sum payments to several publishers including Academic Press, Blackwell and the Institute of Physics. In return universities will be allowed to take out or renew subscriptions to specified journals at well below the list price – with Blackwell for example the journals will be supplied at 60% of normal cost. In addition the licence provides for the free copying and inclusion of articles in study packs without further copyright clearance, and access to the electronic editions when these become available.

Network pricing

A particularly complex issue as far as CD-ROM is concerned is the pricing of site licences enabling multiple access to discs. Some publishers and suppliers will allow their discs to be networked free of charge; most though require extra payment and this is where the complications arise. As one might expect there is no standardisation in pricing policy, with each publisher setting different rates for different types of access. These permutations include:

- the number of users who have access to the CD-ROM. The DSC, for example, charges an annual licence fee of the list price plus 50% for networking their current-alerting service *Inside Information* to 2-12 users. Over 13 users the fee is 100% of the list price. Many suppliers though charge according to the number of simultaneous users, rather than the number of networked terminals, some of which may access the CD-ROM infrequently. SilverPlatter networking fees increase in steps of three, starting at 2-4 simultaneous users and rising to 21 and over.

- the geographical extent of the network – whether use is restricted to a building, a site, or an institution in several separate locations – a potential problem if there are users wanting to connect into the network when they are working from home. One publisher may allow networking free across a single site but charge for multiple site access. Another supplier's charges may depend on the distance between sites – two sites over 20 miles apart for instance may be categorised as different institutions.

Sometimes the cost of networking is so high, that it may be almost as economic to buy two copies of a disc instead. If the cost is prohibitive then another alternative – unless the discs time-out, have to be returned to the publisher or be destroyed – is to circulate the superseded copies to other service points. In fairness to the users though, it should be made clear to them that they are not accessing the most up-to-date information available.

Recurrent expenditure

One question which needs to be asked at the budgeting stage is what on-going costs (if any) will be required to maintain a resource. With journals and other subscription-based material, there is obviously the cost of renewal; finding the money initially to pay for an expensive database may be an achievement itself, but it will need to be matched with recurrent funding in subsequent years. Another factor which needs to be taken into account is inflation. While the cost of living may only be rising by 2 or 3% per annum, the same cannot be said for printed and electronic information – it would be reasonable for instance to estimate for an average 10% increase in journal prices each year. Apart from renewals and inflation, there is also the cost of maintaining equipment and providing consumables, such as paper and toner for printers. While these may not be paid for out of the same fund as information resources, their cost will have to be met from somewhere within the service's budget.

Allocation of funding

Whatever the type of budget and service, decisions will have to be made on how the funding should be allocated. A balance will need to be struck between the competing demands of different subject fields, between different categories of resource, such as books, periodicals and audio-visual materials, and between information in printed and electric format. In a small service with a low budget these decisions might be made as the need arises, avoiding the need to determine in advance how the funding should be divided. In larger organisations the division of the budget will normally be made when the funds become available at the beginning of the financial year.

A number of factors need to be taken into account when allocating a budget. These include:

- past experience, a useful – though not infallible – indicator of future needs. If for instance £1000 was sufficient to cover the costs of on-line searching in the previous financial year, then the fund probably only needs to be increased by a small amount for the coming 12 months

- the level of demand for particular subject fields or types of material – for instance where there are large number of enquiries for business information it will be necessary to invest more heavily in financial directories and databases

- the need to build-up or maintain specific collections, such as a 'jobs section' or 'community information service' provided by many public libraries. To keep such collections up to date, means providing enough money to buy new directories, government publications such as Acts of Parliament and the like

- the need to restrain spending in a specific area or on a certain type of material. In many academic libraries a rough rule of thumb is to keep spending on scientific and technical journals at no more than 60% of the total materials budget – not an easy task with the rise in prices that has taken place over the last few years

- the need to maintain a balance between different sectors and interests. With funding for CD-ROMs, for instance, it is advisable to spread the resources as evenly as possible between subject fields, to ensure all sections are treated fairly.

Other funding arrangements

In some circumstances the funding for an expensive subscription or database may be impossible from the existing budget. If the resource is important enough, it can be worth looking at other possible arrangements, such as:

- additional funding. The possibilities will obviously depend on the environment within which the service operates, but options to consider include bids to central funds and cost-sharing with other sections with a particular interest in a resource. Although the latter approach may seem initially unpromising, there are some success stories – a hospital library for instance which managed to fund the expansion of its CD-ROM service with contributions from departments and by selling a current-awareness database. If the alternative is a patchwork of unsupported databases locked away in offices, then departmental heads might be persuaded to co-operate. One point to bear in mind though is the continuing requirement for funds – while a one-off bid for central funding to buy a new database may be successful, there is still the question of how to find the money for renewal.

- charging fees to defray, either partially or completely, the cost of a resource. Apart from any ideological objections, at a practical level charging may have a detrimental effect on the usage of a resource – one of the reasons for the overwhelming success of CD-ROMs is that the databases have been provided free at the point of use in most services. However if cost recovery is a viable (or the only) option, there are several issues to consider. Are there to be any exemptions or should a fee always be charged? How much ought the charge to be? How should this be levied, for example as a flat rate or on a per page basis? Finally an assessment has to be made on the best time to introduce charges – starting with no fees will make it more difficult to introduce charges at a later stage. On the other hand an introductory period of free use will help to promote a resource or service, giving users an indication of its scope and potential

Though never a popular option, the possibility of cutting back on existing subscriptions should also be considered. If a new journal is needed by a particular group of users, it may be that a large part of the cost could be met by cancelling the order to another periodical in the same subject area. There is always an understandable reluctance to do this, but unless subscriptions are periodically reviewed there will be little scope for new material.

Devolved budgets

In the last few years devolved budgeting – where the money for information resources is controlled not by the library and information service but by the user departments – has become more common, particularly in higher education establishments. In such circumstances the ultimate decision on how to spend the funds rests with the users, or their nominated representatives. There is no doubt that devolved budgeting can present a challenge to a service, and there will inevitably be occasions when a resource which would not have been the librarian's first choice is acquired. However given good liaison and co-operation between the departments and the service the arrangement can be made to work. Users still need (and are usually grateful for) help in finding out about new publications, evaluating and comparing databases, arranging demonstrations, free trials and all the other activities involved in the selection of resources. A vital element for success is a positive, active, and alert approach by the library staff.

Collection development policies

The selection of new resources is only one aspect – albeit a major element – in the provision of information. Although arguably less interesting and satisfying, the reviewing of existing resources, and the weeding out of obsolete or little-used material are also necessary aspects of provision. Together these activities – selection, monitoring and relegation – constitute the collection development process. Over the last decade or so there has been a trend towards establishing formal collection development policies, stating the aims of the selection (and relegation) processes. Some of these statements tend to be vague in nature, along the lines of 'to provide appropriate information for ...'. Others are more specific, including aims such as 'to increase stock availability of material at the time of demand'. An example of a very clear and well-presented policy is that produced by Birmingham Library Services, which has published a series of leaflets for users outlining the aims of their stock selection techniques (Figure 1).

There is an argument that policy statements are not worth the paper they are written on and that the time involved could be spent more productivly. However there are points in favour of establishing a policy, not least of which is that it helps concentrate the mind on the long term planning of resources. At a practical level it is important that if a policy is drawn up, this should be established in conjunction with the users of a service. Developing a policy by the library and information staff alone could well lead to 'ivory tower' statements not in accordance with the users' needs.

Monitoring use

In terms of monitoring techniques, there are a number of ways of keeping a watch on the amount of use a resource receives. The most obvious example is the date label in loan copies; with printed reference works it is possible to get a good idea from the number of enquiries for which it has been used, from the state of the material – dog-eared or pristine condition – or whether the item goes missing. For journals an assessment might involve fastening a label on the front cover of each issue or a survey in which users allocate 'votes' to all titles they consider useful (Figure 2). Monitoring the usage of electronic resources can often be done automatically – with CD-ROM networks for example there are software packages available which will keep statistics on which databases have been consulted. If a booking system is in use, manual statistics can also be compiled from the daily signing sheets. The methods devised will depend on the type and size of service but they are vital to maintain the dynamic nature of the collection.

Introducing Stock Selection

Our Aim
Birmingham Library Services exists to provide, promote and encourage access to information and imagination through books, print and other forms of communication

Our main activity is the provision of books and the promotion of the benefit and enjoyment of reading for all groups in the community. Books are unique as a means to communicate information, ideas and knowledge.

Setting the standards
We want to offer a stock which reflects a broad range of views on all sorts of subjects:
- we will keep within the law
- we will not suppress material simply because it "gives offence"
- we will seek to provide accurate and up-to-date information
- we will act on policies formulated by the city council.

As a public service we are here to serve the needs of the whole community- equally. All Birmingham citizens, but especially those who are disadvantaged or do not often use libraries have the right to expect imaginative stock provision suited to their needs. Our goal is to offer a range of books and materials which reflect the cultural origins and interests of the city's diverse communities.

Why do we need to select?
Some 78,000 titles are published each year in Britain alone. Even in a city as large as Birmingham it is impossible for us to buy every one. Choices have to be made.

What is a good book?
These are some of the questions we ask when assessing a book:
- Will it get much use?
- Will interest in it last?
- It is well produced and attractively presented?
- Is it well printed and illustrated?
- Is there a demand for this subject?
- Is there need for updated copy?
- Is the information accurate and up to date?
- Is the author well-known?
- Will it help to offer a better choice on the shelves?
- Are all cultures and lifestyles portrayed positively?

Creating a balance
Purchasing is planned to ensure a continuous supply of new books throughout the year. Each year every library plans its buying by matching the money available against the need for new stock in particular categories: information books, children's picture books, large print and books in community languages for example.

How do we buy our books?
Much of our selection is done from 'approval displays' provided by our supplier but we also purchase from lists, suppliers' showrooms and specialist booksellers. Whichever method is used, you can be sure that books are chosen by librarians who are well aware of their customers' needs.

*Figure 1 – Stock Selection Policy: Reproduced by
kind permission of Birmingham Library Services*

Library and Information Service Review of
Periodical Subscriptions for the School of Engineering

The last review of library periodical subscriptions took place over 4 years ago. Costs have continued to rise annually since then well above increases in library funds.

Following discussions during 1995 it was agreed at School Board that a survey of staff would be undertaken to identify which periodicals currently taken by the Library were still required in order to:

a) address the growing imbalance between spending on books and periodicals (30%/70% in favour of periodicals in 1994/95, 28%-72% projected for this year)

b) allow the purchase of new titles

c) best reflect the requirements of current teaching and research.

The current financial situation makes it likely that we will also have to fund the two main Engineering CD-ROM databases – Inspec and Compendex – from within this budget next financial year.

Attached to this memo is a list of the current subscriptions for your School this year with prices for the last two years. We would like you to indicate which titles you wish to support – and the strength of your support – by distributing 100 "votes" among them. A second list is attached of titles which have been recently reccommended for purchase. You may also wish to allocate votes to these titles. If you wish to vote for titles which are not on either list please write them in at the end. You may vote for as many or as few titles as you wish. There are no restrictions on how you distribute the 100 votes among the titles you support.

Finally, please make sure you write your name at the end of the list and return it to the Nelson Library by Friday 1st March 1996. The results of the survey will be presented to the next School Board.

Figure 2 – Monitoring use: Reproduced by kind permission of
Staffordshire University Library and Information Service

Innovation

When some-one is new to resource selection the normal tendency is to proceed with great caution. There are no built-in yardsticks against which to measure a new purchase – no prior knowledge of comparable products or opinions on what would be a reasonable cost for a resource. The fear of making an expensive mistake can loom very large in the mind. Now that the pace of technological change is so fast with so many new sources of information appearing, there is also the risk that something better will be available in a few months time. Although it is right to be wary, it is also possible to be too cautious. Some risks are inevitable in resource selection – there is no way of knowing for certain in advance that everything acquired will be used on a regular basis. Equally it is not always feasible to wait indefinitely for the 'right' product. There will not be many thanks for delaying – better to accept the occasional mistake and have a dynamic resource collection responding to the users' needs, than a service with out of date information and obsolete equipment.

9. Sources of further information

Books

Bradley, P. *UKOLUG Quick Guide to the Internet*. London, United Kingdom Online User Group, 1995.

Dickinson, G K. *Selection and Evaluation of Electronic Resources*. Englewood, Colarado, Libraries Unlimited, 1994.

McKay, D. *Effective Financial Management of Library and Information Services*. London, Aslib, 1995. (Aslib Know How Guide)

Morley, M and Woodward, H. (eds). *Taming the Electronic Jungle: Electronic Information: The Collection Management Issues.* National Acquisitions Group and the UK Serials Group, 1993.

Spiller, D. *Book Selection: Principles and Practice*. 5th ed. London, Library Association, 1991.

Stoker, D. *Electronic Information Sources: an evaluative guide*. London, Bowker-Saur, 1996

Woodward, H and Morley, M. *Endangered Species?: Evolving Strategies for Library Collection Management*.United Kingdom Serials Group and National Acquisitions Group, 1995.

Articles

Dade, P. Pilot trial of Blackwell's *UnCover* database. *Vine* 98 (March 1995) 40-2.

Gillham, M. What makes a good multimedia CD-ROM? *Managing Information* 2(12) December 1995 38-40.

McMahon, K. Using the BUBL information service as an Internet reference resource. *Managing Information* 2 (4) 1995 33-35.

McMurdo, G. How the Internet was indexed. *Journal of Information Science.* 21(6) 1995 479-489.

Medawar, K. Database quality: a literature review of the past and a plan for the future. *Program*, 29 (3) July 1995, 257-272.

Mendelsohn, S. Evaluating Databases. *Information World Review*, June 1996, 28-29.

Rowley, J and Butcher, D. Pricing strategies for business information on CD-ROM. *Journal of Information Science* 22(1) 1996 39-46.

Woodward, H. The impact of electronic information on serials collection management. *Serials* 7(1) March 1994 29-36.

Yeardon, J. Experience with SilverPlatter Electronic Reference Library at Imperial College. *Program* 29(2) April 1995 169-175.

Organisations

National Acquisitions Group (NAG)
Westfield House
North Road, Horsforth,
Leeds, LS18 5HG
Tel: +44 (0) 113 259 1447
Fax: +44 (0) 113 259 1447
Email: *swolf@nag.eunet.co.uk*

The Group's membership includes individuals and organisations within publishing and bookselling, as well as librarians responsible for buying books for all types of services. Activities include an annual conference, seminars and visits, plus the publication of *NAG News* and *Taking Stock*, a twice yearly journal.

OCLC Europe
7th Floor, Tricorn House
51-53 Hagley Road
Birmingham B16 8TP
Tel: +44 (0) 121 456 4656
Fax: +44 (0) 121 456 4680

Silver Platter Information Ltd.
10 Barley Mow Passage
Chiswick
London W4 4PH
Tel: +44 (0) 181 995 8242
Fax: +44 (0) 181 995 5159

United Kingdom Serials Group
c/o Jill Tolson
UKSG Administrator
114 Woodstock Road
Witney OX8 6DY

Tel: +44 (0) 1993 703 466
Fax: +44 (0) 1993 778 879
Email: *uksg@bham.ac.uk*

The UKSG was established to encourage the exchange and promotion of ideas on printed and electronic serials. The Group runs courses, holds an annual conference and publishes *Serials: the Journal of the United Kingdom Serials Group.*

Internet Search Tools

AltaVista   *http://altavista.digital.com/*

Lycos   *http://lycos.cs.cmu.edu*

Yahoo   *http://www.yahoo.com*

BUBL Information Service
Dennis Nicholson,
Andersonian Library, University of Strathclyde,
101 St James' Road, Glasgow, G4 0NS.
Tel: +44 (0) 141 552 3701ext 4632/4618
Fax: +44 (0) 141 552 3304 (mark FAO: BUBL)
URL: *http://www.bubl.bath.ac.uk/BUBL/home.html*

SOSIG (Social Sciences Gateway)
Centre for Computing in the Social Sciences
University of Bristol
8 Woodland Road
Bristol BS8 1TN
Tel: +44 (0) 117 928 8478
Fax: +44 (0) 117 928 8473
Email: *sosig-info@bris.ac.uk*
URL: *http://sosig.esrc.bris.ac.uk/*

Project EARL
4th Floor, Gun Court,
70 Wapping Lane
London E1 9RL
Tel: +44 (0) 171 702 2020
Fax: +44 (0) 171 702 2019
Email: *info@earl.org.uk*
URL: *http://www.earl.org.uk/earl*